RACHEL KHOO'S
muesli & granola

WEIDENFELD & NICOLSON

RACHEL KHOO'S
muesli & granola

WEIDENFELD & NICOLSON

This edition published in Great Britain in 2013 by Weidenfeld & Nicolson
Originally published in 2010 by Hachette Livre – Marabout
Text © Rachel Khoo 2013
Design and layout © Weidenfeld & Nicolson 2013
ISBN: 978 0 2978 6893 4

10 9 8 7 6 5 4 3 2 1

Photography by Akiko Ida
Food styling by Rachel Khoo
Prop styling by Élodie Rambaud
Design by Kate Barr
English translation by Isabel Varea for Ros Schwartz Translations Ltd

A CIP catalogue record for this book is available from the British Library.

The Orion Publishing Group's policy is to use papers that are natural, renewable
and recyclable and made from wood grown in sustainable forests. The logging
and manufacturing processes are expected to conform to the environmental regulations of the
country of origin.

Printed and bound in China.

Weidenfeld & Nicolson
The Orion Publishing Group Ltd
Orion House
5 Upper St Martin's Lane
London WC2H 9EA

An Hachette UK Company

www.orionbooks.co.uk

contents

foreword

When I embarked on writing my first cookery book in 2009, I had been living in Paris for four years. By then, even though Paris had started to feel like home, I still craved my home comforts.

The typical French breakfast consisting of a strong black coffee and croissant just didn't cut the mustard and getting some decent bacon for a proper English fry up just wasn't possible (and equally not something I tend to crave everyday). I wanted to continue the longstanding Breakfast ritual I had started while living in London (the city where I had spent most of my life before moving to Paris); a pot of steaming tea with a bowl of nutritious muesli. In Paris, tea was easier to come by thanks to the envelopes stuffed with English tea that Mum would pop in the post. Getting hold of some decent muesli, on the other hand, was a far more challenging feat. Most of the stuff I found resembled a bag of sawdust where, as if by accident, the odd nut or piece of shriveled up fruit had ended up in.

And hence, my muesli mission was born. I scoured the town high and low for different kinds of oats, grains, nuts and dried fruit – which led me to start drying my own fruit (see recipe on page 24). I roasted, stirred, grinded and baked every possible muesli-related concoction. My studio apartment was no longer my home, but a miniature muesli making factory. I took over friends' places to host muesli and granola parties where they would taste test my latest creations and then vote for their favourite. Out of the muesli madness I wrote this book, which is quite simply, my collection of muesli, granola and muesli bars recipes – with a few added bonuses along the way.

The daughter of a Malaysian Chinese father and an Austrian mother, Rachel grew up in Croydon before graduating from Central Saint Martin's College of Art and Design in London. Ultimately, her passion for patisserie lured her to Paris, where she studied at Le Cordon Bleu and became a pastry chef and cook.

First published in French as *Barres à Cereals: Granola et Muesli Maison*, this collection of recipes is her first book. Rachel's culinary life in Paris was the subject of the TV series and bestselling cookery book, *The Little Paris Kitchen*.

THE BASICS

oats, etc.

Oats are the traditional base for muesli, granola and porridge. Even so, you can use many other cereals, such as millet, spelt, quinoa and rice. These add taste and texture and can be used to complement or replace oats.

shopping for oats

When you buy oats or any other cereal, always read the label to see whether sugar, salt or artificial flavourings have been added. Go for 'natural' products and sweeten them to your own taste.

tips

To release the best possible flavour from oats, toast gently in a large, non-stick frying pan for around 3–4 minutes until golden. If you are preparing a large quantity, toast 100g/3½oz at a time as the flakes will cook unevenly if you put too many in the pan at once.

cooking

You can toast a mixture of cereal flakes, such as oats, barley, millet, buckwheat or rice, together. If you are short of time, buy packets of ready-toasted mixed cereals.

storage

Unopened packets of toasted oats will keep for at least six weeks. Store in an airtight container in a cool, dry place.

oats

There are many health benefits from eating oats. They reduce cholesterol and are a good source of fibre, vitamin E, zinc, selenium, copper, iron, manganese and magnesium – the list goes on. Oats contain slight traces of gluten and should be avoided by people with a severe gluten allergy. Oats are usually sold as flakes; the oat grains are dehusked, then steamed and flattened.

different types of oats

Porridge oats are best for making smooth, creamy porridge that's ideal for babies. Small oat flakes can be used for any cereal-based dish; the bigger the flakes, the thicker the porridge. Large oat flakes are less processed and therefore contain more nutrients. They are better for granola and muesli than for porridge as they are usually much firmer. Quick-cook oats only take 2–3 minutes to cook, but they undergo a longer manufacturing process and are less nutritious than other types. Their taste is rather bland and their texture not as appealing as less processed oats.

1 . millet
2 . barley
3 . spelt flakes
4 . quinoa
5 . puffed rice
6 . rice
7 . buckwheat

millet

Millet is a tasty cereal with a slightly sweet, nutty flavour. It contains a whole series of nutrients including vitamin B, potassium, phosphorus, magnesium, iron, zinc, copper and manganese. While it is not as rich in proteins as wheat, it is still a good source. It's also gluten-free and ideal for those with wheat allergies.

barley

Barley has a very similar nutritional value to wheat. However, it is richer in fibre, essential fatty acids, vitamin E (wheat contains very little) and other nutrients, making it a more nourishing cereal. Like oats, barley contains traces of gluten.

spelt

A nutty, highly nutritious cereal with a very long history. Spelt comes from a plant similar to wheat, with slightly longer and more pointed grains. It contains a wide variety of nutrients and is an excellent source of vitamin B2 and a good source of manganese, niacin, thiamine and copper.

quinoa

Like buckwheat, quinoa is technically not a cereal but the fruit of a plant of the chenopodiacea family, which also includes spinach and Swiss chard. Quinoa is regarded as a 'superfood'. It contains a number of nutrients and is among those rare foods that have an ideal protein balance and is also high in polyunsaturates. Make sure to store it in an airtight container away from light and heat. Quinoa is gluten-free so is suitable for those who are gluten intolerant.

puffed rice

Puffed rice livens up any bowl of cereal. Buy it unsweetened so you can control for yourself the amount of sugar used. Rice contains no gluten and can be enjoyed by people with gluten allergies.

rice

Short-grain or risotto rice is best for making congee (savoury rice porridge or rice pudding). It's able to absorb liquids and is better at releasing starch, making your porridge or pudding creamier than the long-grain variety.

buckwheat

Buckwheat has a pleasant, rich flavour all its own. Being gluten-free, it presents no problems for people with coeliac disease. It technically isn't a cereal but the fruit of a flowering plant belonging to the polygonaceae family. It's full of protein and B vitamins, and rich in phosphorus, potassium, iron, calcium and lysine. An excellent source of dietary fibre, it helps reduce cholesterol.

15

types of sugar

Just how much sugar you add to a mixture of cereals depends on the ingredients. As a rule, there's no need to add sugar if the mix includes a lot of dried fruit, which are fairly rich in natural sugars. Otherwise, ½–1 tsp is usually enough.

white, golden and dark brown

From a nutritional point of view, there's not much difference between refined white, golden or dark brown sugar. The golden or dark brown types contain certain minerals, especially calcium, potassium, iron and magnesium, while white sugar contains none of these.

However, golden and dark brown sugar have no real health benefits since the minerals are only present in minute quantities. The real difference lies in their flavour and how they affect oven-baked dishes. Golden and dark brown sugar not only have a richer taste but are also more moist than white sugar, making them ideal for baking and for producing deliciously smooth desserts.

palm

Palm sugar is produced by boiling the sap of the sugar palm tree to a syrup until it reaches a caramel-like consistency. The syrup is left to cool and then moulded into blocks. To use the block sugar you only have to grate it. Palm sugar has a subtle flavour of hazelnuts and caramel.

Sweetening power: a little higher than ordinary sugar; 1 tbsp white sugar is equivalent to ¾ tbsp palm sugar. *Where to find it:* at Chinese or Indian grocers' shops – it's very cheap.

agave syrup

Agave syrup, sometimes called agave nectar, is produced from the agave plant. The sap of the plant is reduced to obtain a syrup slightly thinner than honey. The syrup provides a constant supply of energy and has a low glycaemic index. It's much sweeter than sugar, so you need less of it.

Sweetening power: 1 tbsp white sugar is equivalent to ½ tbsp agave syrup. *Where to find it:* on sale in health-food shops or online.

maple syrup

Maple syrup is a sweetener obtained from the sap of the maple tree. Its nutty flavour makes it the perfect accompaniment to a bowl of nice hot porridge.

Sweetening power: four times sweeter than ordinary sugar; 4 tbsp sugar are equivalent to 1 tbsp maple syrup.

golden syrup

Golden syrup is made from the juice of the sugar cane with a flavour similar to maple syrup combined with caramel and a hint of honey. To make it easier to extract from the tin, pour some boiling water into a bowl and stand the golden syrup tin in the water for 5 minutes – or, better still, buy your golden syrup in a squeezy bottle.

Sweetening power: stronger than ordinary sugar; 1 tbsp sugar equals ¾ tbsp golden syrup.

honey

Honey is great for sweetening cereals. It also ensures that granola and muesli bars hold together. *(Warning: Honey is unsuitable for infants less than 12 months old as it is a potential source of botulism. The botulism spores can germinate and multiply, releasing a toxin that can prove highly dangerous for small babies.)*

1

2

3

1. white sugar
2. palm sugar
3. agave syrup
4. maple syrup
5. golden syrup
6. golden caster sugar
7. dark brown sugar

milk, etc.

The Swiss Doctor Maximilian Bircher-Benner, inventor of muesli (see recipe page 40), used to serve it with condensed milk because, in the 1900s, pasteurisation and refrigeration were not widespread. Nowadays, cow's milk is only one of many options.

soya milk

Soya milk is obtained from soy beans. It contains neither lactose, gluten nor cholesterol and has almost the same percentage of proteins as cow's milk, although it is lower in fat. Shop-bought soya milk often contains an oil emulsion to stabilise the milk, as well as other additives. If you make your own, you can be sure you are drinking pure soya milk.

makes 1 litre • preparation time: 30 minutes • soaking time: 8 hours or overnight • cooking time: 15 minutes

150g/5½oz soy beans (available from Asian or Chinese grocers or in healthfood shops)
1.75 litres/3 pints mineral or filtered water
Pinch salt
Sugar, honey, maple or agave syrup or 2 dried dates, to sweeten

Rinse the soy beans several times in cold water. Leave them to soak overnight in 500ml/17fl oz mineral or filtered water.

Drain the soy beans and rinse them again. Discard the hulls that have come away from the beans. Put the beans in a blender with 1.25 litres/28fl oz water and blend, not too finely, for about a minute. Press the mixture through a very fine sieve or a clean coffee filter to extract the milk. Discard the soy bean pulp.

Pour the soya milk into a saucepan, bring to the boil, then continue to boil for about 10 minutes. Add salt and sugar to taste. If you are adding dried dates, remove the stones, then place them in the blender with the milk and blend until smooth.Leave to cool before pouring into an airtight container. The milk will keep in the refrigerator for one week.

nut milk

Nut milk can be made from almost any kind of nut and is as simple to prepare as soya milk. There's no cooking involved, so none of the nuts' nutritional benefits are lost. The milk will have a strong taste of nuts, so choose your favourite variety. If you prefer, use a mixture.

makes 1 litre / 1 ¾ pints • preparation time: 30 minutes • soaking time: 8 hours or overnight

350g / 12oz nuts (unsalted, shelled but not skinned)
1.25 litres / 28fl oz mineral or filtered water
Pinch salt
Sugar, honey, maple or agave syrup or 2 dried dates, to sweeten

Rinse the nuts several times in cold water. Leave them to soak overnight in the mineral or filtered water. Pour the mixture into a blender, then blend for 1–2 minutes or until the blender becomes less noisy. The mixture should not be too fine.

Press the mixture through a very fine sieve or a clean coffee filter to extract the nut milk. Keep the pulp to use later, for example in a crumble (see page 116) or a 'no-cook' muesli bar (see page 87).

Add salt and sugar to taste. If you are adding dried dates, remove the stones, then place in the blender with the milk and blend until smooth. Pour into an airtight container. The milk will keep in the refrigerator for one week.

coconut milk

Coconut milk is the rich white liquid obtained by pressing grated coconut flesh through a sieve with hot water. If you can't get hold of fresh coconuts, simply buy a packet of grated or shredded coconut or frozen or powdered coconut.

---

makes 1 litre/1¾ pints • preparation time: 15 minutes • soaking time: 5 hours

---

2 litres/3½ pints mineral or filtered water
500g/1lb 2oz grated coconut, unsweetened
Pinch salt
Sugar, honey, maple or agave syrup or 2 dried dates, to sweeten

Bring the water to the boil in a saucepan. Pour the boiling water over the coconut and leave to cool for about 5 minutes.

Press the coconut mixture through a fine sieve or a clean coffee filter to extract the milk. Discard the pulp and pour the coconut milk into a container. Add salt and sugar to taste. If you are adding dried dates, remove the stones, then place in the blender with the coconut and blend until smooth.

Pour the milk into an airtight container. It will keep in the refrigerator for up to one week.

dried fruit

Dried fruits are like nature's own 'sweets'. They have the added bonus of containing antioxidants and vitamins and none of the goodness of the fruit is lost during the drying process. Dried fruits make great snacks for adults and children and are delicious added to muesli or granola.

shop-bought dried fruit

Dried fruit sold commercially often contains added sugar and sulphurous anhydride – a gas used to preserve the fruit's bright colour. If you buy dried fruit at the supermarket, check the use-by date and the ingredients. Buy fruit without added sugar or preservatives, with as long a use-by date as possible. But why buy them when you can make your own?

when you buy fresh fruit

Make sure they have no blemishes and aren't too ripe.

preparing fruit for drying

Wash and dry the fruit carefully. Remove stones or pips, leaves and stalks. Peel the fruit if you wish, then cut into slices of equal size. Small fruit or berries can be left whole. Remember that the larger and juicier the fruit, the longer it will take to dry. Even so, don't cut the pieces small as they will shrink by around 60 per cent as they dry. Dissolve 1 tsp crushed soluble vitamin C tablet(s) in 250ml/8½fl oz water. Dip the sliced fruit in the liquid. This will help it to retain its colour.

drying fruit in the oven

Preheat the oven to the lowest possible temperature (70–90°C/180°F/Gas mark ¼). Line a baking tray with greaseproof paper. Spread the fruit over the tray and place in the oven. According to the type of fruit, the drying process will take between 4–6 hours.

It is important to dehydrate the fruit correctly to eliminate all bacteria. To make sure this has been done, touch the pieces of fruit after you take them out of the oven. They should be dry – but not brittle – and soft, with a leathery texture. Cut off a piece of dried fruit and look carefully at the cut surface. If it is still moist, it's not yet done. For a chewier texture, leave the fruit in the oven for a little longer.

food dehydrator
A dehydrator is a machine that dries fruit, vegetables, herbs and meat using very little energy (less than a conventional oven) and taking up minimal space.

There are different types: top-of-the-range professional models with drawers and temperature control and more basic versions for domestic use with stackable trays and usually no temperature control. If you are a beginner in drying fruit, a basic model should be fine. Each type of fruit requires a different drying time – refer to the instruction manual.

storage
Keep dried fruit in an airtight container in a cool, dry place. Put the container in a paper bag to protect the fruit from the daylight. If you prefer to refrigerate dried fruit, make sure it is in an airtight container, otherwise it may go mouldy in the damp environment of the refrigerator. Dried fruit will keep for at least one month.

nuts & seeds

No wonder nutritionists proclaim the benefits of nuts and seeds for the brain.
They're jam-packed with antioxidants, essential fatty acids (omega-3 and omega-6),
proteins and fibre and contain all the nutrients necessary for the wellbeing of the
body as a whole and the nervous system in particular.

tips
Buy whole nuts, with the skin on, rather than chopped ones,
which will lose some of their flavour if stored for too long.

Keep nuts in airtight containers in the freezer
or refrigerator to prevent them turning rancid.

To bring out the flavour of nuts and seeds, toast them
in a dry frying pan for 2 minutes before using.

**Always buy unsalted nuts; salted ones are unsuitable
for the recipes in this book.**

nuts that are great with muesli and granola
almonds, hazelnuts, macadamia nuts, pecans, Brazil nuts,
cashews, pistachios, coconut.

seeds that are perfect for muesli and granola
sunflower, pumpkin, poppy, sesame (golden or black) and flax seeds
(golden or brown).

*Some healthfood shops sell packets of mixed seeds, so you don't need
to buy several different packs.*

2

7

6

1

3

5

11

9

8

12

10

4

1. hazelnuts
2. sesame seeds
3. walnuts
4. pumpkin seeds
5. sunflower seeds
6. poppy seeds
7. brown flax seeds
8. pecans
9. cashew nuts
10. macadamia nuts
11. coconut
12. Brazil nuts

fruit compotes

Liven up your breakfast muesli or porridge by adding some fruit compote. Compotes can also be a basic ingredient in granola or a crumble.

A bit of advice: make the compote at least a day in advance to give the flavours time to develop. If you are making compote for a baby, omit the sugar, spices and herbs.

apple compote with cinnamon

preparation time: 10 minutes • cooking time: 15 minutes

1 lemon
6 large apples, peeled, cored and cut into eighths
50g/1¾oz golden caster sugar or other sweetener
1 cinnamon stick or 1 tsp ground cinnamon

Squeeze the lemon into a bowl. Place the apple pieces into the bowl and stir with the lemon juice. Put the sugar and cinnamon in a saucepan and place over a medium heat.

Let the sugar dissolve and brown slightly before stirring in the apples and lemon juice. Cook for 10–15 minutes until the apples are soft. Remove the cinnamon stick, if used. Serve hot or leave to cool before placing in the refrigerator in an airtight container.

nectarine compote with basil

preparation time: 10 minutes • cooking time: 15 minutes

5 nectarines
50g/1¾oz white sugar or sweetener of your choice
50ml/1½fl oz water
1 bunch basil

Cut the nectarines into small pieces and place in a saucepan with the sugar and water. Cover and cook over a low heat until soft. Add the chopped basil (with the stalks). Gently crush the nectarines and basil to achieve a smoother consistency. Serve hot or leave to cool before placing in the refrigerator in an airtight container.

plum & ginger compote

preparation time: 10 minutes • cooking time: 30 minutes

5 6 large plums, washed, halved and stones removed
1 tsp fresh ginger, finely grated
½ tsp ground ginger
50g/1¾oz palm sugar

Wash the plums, cut them in half and remove the stones. Place the grated ginger in a large frying pan with the ground ginger and sugar. Fry over a medium heat until golden. Add the plum halves, flesh side down. Cook for 20–30 minutes or until soft. Serve hot or leave to cool before placing in the refrigerator in an airtight container. Hint: use a spoon to peel the fresh ginger – it's much easier.

grapefruit & orange compote

preparation time: 5 minutes • cooking time: 30 minutes

5 oranges (unwaxed)
3 grapefruits (unwaxed)
100g/3½oz honey

Place the zest of 1 orange and 1 grapefruit in a large frying pan.
Place the oranges and grapefruits on a chopping board. Cut off both
ends of the fruit to expose the flesh. This helps the fruit to stay in place
and not roll about. Take one of the pieces of fruit in your hand. Starting
at the top, cut the peel and pith into strips, following the natural curve
of the fruit.

When you have removed all the peel, hold the fruit firmly in your hand over
a bowl and gently slide the blade of a knife along each membrane towards the
centre of the fruit to separate it into segments. Pull the segments away from the
fruit and put them in the bowl. Repeat the operation with the rest of the fruit.

Pour the juice from the bowl into the frying pan with the zest. Add the honey
and place the frying pan over a medium heat. Cook for about 20 minutes until
the liquid turns golden and syrupy. Pour the syrup over the fruit and stir
thoroughly. Pour the mixture into an airtight container and refrigerate.

rhubarb compote

600g/1lb 5oz rhubarb
75g/2¾oz golden caster sugar

Preheat the oven to 180°C/350°F/Gas mark 4. Cut the rhubarb into 5cm/2in pieces, then rinse in a colander. Spread the rhubarb over an ovenproof dish and sprinkle with the sugar. Mix thoroughly, then place in the oven. After about 15 minutes, remove from the oven, stir again, then return to the oven. The rhubarb should be soft and beginning to fall apart after 25 30 minutes. Serve the compote hot or leave to cool before placing in the refrigerator in an airtight container.

apricot & date compote with rose water

300g/10½oz dried apricots
40g/1½oz pistachios, shelled
2 tbsp honey
2 tbsp rose water
300ml/½ pint boiling water
200g/7oz dried dates

Put the apricots, pistachios, honey and rose water in a saucepan and pour the boiling water over them. Leave to soak for at least 4 hours or overnight. Before serving, cut the dried dates in half and add them to the compote.

MUESLI

muesli base

Here's my own recipe. The big advantage of making your own muesli is that you can use whatever ingredients you fancy. Adding powdered milk produces a creamier texture. Experiment with different sorts and sizes of oats. But don't stop there – add chopped fresh fruit, or fruit compote. It's delicious.

serves 1 • preparation time: 5 minutes • cooking time: 3 minutes

1 tbsp chopped nuts
6 tbsp oats
1 tbsp mixed seeds (sunflower, sesame, poppy or flax)
1 tsp golden caster sugar or sweetener of your choice
2 tbsp dried fruit, chopped
1 tsp powdered milk
Pinch salt

Toast the nuts, oats and seeds in a dry frying pan for 2–3 minutes or until they turn golden. Stir them into the remaining ingredients. Serve with milk or yogurt.

Muesli base will keep in an airtight container for several months. That's if you can resist it that long …

bircher muesli

Dr Bircher used to serve muesli as a light meal with a cup of tea and a slice of buttered wholemeal bread. Unlike packet muesli, which is mostly cereal, Bircher muesli contains lots of fruit. This recipe differs slightly from the original with the addition of sultanas and orange juice and yogurt instead of full cream.

*serves 1 • preparation time: **5 minutes** • soaking time: **8 hours***

3 tbsp oats
1 tbsp sultanas
Juice of 1 orange
1 apple (about 150g/5½oz)
2 tbsp yogurt
1 tbsp honey
1 tbsp hazelnuts, chopped

Soak the oats and sultanas in the orange juice for 8 hours or overnight. Grate the apple (including the peel) and stir into the oat mixture with the yogurt. Drizzle with honey and garnish with the chopped hazelnuts.

Eat immediately.

41

muesli

english muesli

I often ate this when visiting my grandmother. She made vast quantities that she stored in large plastic containers. The bran flakes add a pleasant crunchiness.

serves 1 • preparation time: 5 minutes • cooking time: 3 minutes

8 tbsp oats
2 tbsp bran flakes or other flakes
2 tbsp sultanas
1 tsp powdered milk
1 tsp golden caster sugar
Pinch salt

Toast the oats in a dry frying pan for 2–3 minutes or until they turn golden. Leave to cool slightly. Stir all the ingredients together.

Serve with milk or yogurt.

winter muesli

Cinnamon and ginger go very well with apples and add a touch of warmth to a version of muesli that's just right for cold days. It's also fantastic with a generous spoonful of apple compote (see page 30).

serves 1 • preparation time: 5 minutes • cooking time: 3 minutes

2 tbsp chopped nuts
6 tbsp oats
2 tbsp mixed seeds
1 tsp golden caster sugar or sweetener of your choice
½ tsp ground cinnamon
Pinch ground ginger
3 tbsp dried apples, chopped
1 tsp powdered milk
Pinch salt

Toast the nuts, oats and seeds in a dry frying pan for 2–3 minutes or until they turn golden. Leave to cool slightly. Stir all the ingredients together.

Serve with milk or yogurt.

very chocolatey muesli

This recipe is dedicated to all chocoholics frustrated by the poor quality of chocolate breakfast cereals. It's loaded with chocolate in a variety of forms including cocoa powder, chocolate cereals (I use chocolate rice puffs but you can use any that you fancy), chocolate from a bar and cacao nibs (roasted and shelled cocoa beans).

serves 1 • preparation time: 3 minutes • cooking time: 5 minutes

6 tbsp oats
2 tbsp chocolate cereal
1 tsp golden caster sugar
1 tsp cocoa powder
2 tbsp chocolate, chopped
1 tbsp cacao nibs, chopped
Pinch salt

Toast the oats in a dry frying pan for 2–3 minutes or until they turn golden. Leave to cool. Stir all the ingredients together.

Serve with milk or yogurt.

muesli with nuts & seeds

This hearty muesli will go down well with fans of nuts and seeds. It uses powdered almond milk instead of cow's milk and sugar. For a crunchier texture, try using coconut flakes instead of desiccated coconut.

serves 1 • preparation time: 3 minutes • cooking time: 5 minutes

6 tbsp mixed buckwheat
and large oats
2 tbsp cereal flakes of your choice
1 tbsp hazelnuts, chopped
1 tbsp pecans, chopped
1 tbsp flaked almonds
1 tsp pumpkin seeds

1 tsp sunflower seeds
1 tsp sesame seeds
1 tsp flax seeds
1 tbsp desiccated coconut
1 tsp powdered almond milk
1 tsp maple syrup
Pinch salt

Toast the oats, nuts and seeds in a dry frying pan for 2–3 minutes or until they turn golden. Leave to cool slightly. Stir all the ingredients together apart from the maple syrup.

Serve with milk or yogurt and drizzle the maple syrup on top.

super-energy muesli

*This muesli is brimful of nutrients. Oat flakes are slow-release carbohydrates
that will keep you feeling full until lunchtime. Also in the mix is puffed quinoa,
an excellent source of protein. The dried dates and figs are rich in natural sugar,
potassium and iron, while the nuts and seeds contain omega-3 essential fatty acids.*

serves 1 • preparation time: 3 minutes • cooking time: 5 minutes

5 tbsp oats
2 tbsp cereal flakes of your choice (buckwheat, bran, rye)
2 tbsp puffed quinoa
1 dried date, chopped
1 dried fig, chopped
1 tbsp nuts, chopped
1 tsp pumpkin seeds
1 tsp sunflower seeds
1 tsp flax seeds
1 tsp sesame seeds
1 tsp powdered milk
Pinch salt

Toast the oats, cereal, nuts and seeds in a dry frying pan for 2–3 minutes
or until they turn golden. Leave to cool slightly.

Stir all the ingredients together. Serve with milk or yogurt.

gluten-free muesli

There's nothing complicated about making gluten-free muesli. All you need is a quick visit to a healthfood shop where you'll find all the necessary ingredients. Don't forget to read the labels.

*serves 1 • preparation time: **5 minutes** • cooking time: **3 minutes***

4 tbsp buckwheat oats
2 tbsp buckwheat flakes
2 tbsp puffed rice
2 tbsp puffed quinoa
1 tbsp mixed seeds
1 tsp golden caster sugar or sweetener of your choice
2 tbsp dried fruit, chopped
1 tbsp nuts, chopped
1 tsp powdered milk
Pinch salt

Toast the cereals and seeds in a dry frying pan for 2–3 minutes or until they turn golden. Leave to cool slightly.

Stir all the ingredients together. Serve with milk or yogurt.

muesli

muesli with berries

As the name suggests, this muesli is packed with berries.

6 tbsp oats
2 tbsp cereal flakes of your choice
2 tbsp puffed quinoa
1 tbsp mixed seeds
1 tbsp dried strawberries
1 tbsp dried cherries
1 tbsp dried cranberries
1 tsp powdered milk
Pinch salt
A few fresh berries

Toast the oats, cereals and seeds in a dry frying pan for 2–3 minutes or until they turn golden. Leave to cool slightly.

Mix together all the ingredients, except the fresh berries. Serve with milk or yogurt and garnish with the fresh berries.

exotic muesli

A breakfast-time escape to a tropical island.

serves 1 • preparation time: 5 minutes • cooking time: 3 minutes

6 tbsp oats
Juice of ½ lime
½ banana, sliced
1 tbsp dried pineapple
1 tbsp desiccated coconut
1 tbsp dried mango
1 tbsp dried papaya
1 tbsp Brazil nuts, chopped
1 tsp powdered milk
Pinch salt

Toast the oat flakes in a dry frying pan for 2–3 minutes or until they turn golden.
Leave to cool slightly.

Mix the lime juice with the sliced banana. Mix the oat flakes with the rest
of the ingredients. Serve with milk or yogurt.

GRANOLA

granola base

No need to be a three-star chef to make granola. It's very simple. Just be sure not to add the dried fruit to the oats mixture after you've cooked it, otherwise the fruit will burn. Check the oats regularly as they cook as they can burn in a matter of seconds. I first spotted apple compote being used in a granola recipe in a Nigella Lawson cookbook. My own view is that any fruit compote will work just as well. If you like your granola less sugary, use a fruit compote that is less sweet.

---

makes about 1kg/2¼lb • preparation time: 10 minutes • cooking time: 45 minutes

---

oat base
5 quantities Muesli with Nuts & Seeds
(see recipe page 49)

alternative base
300g/10½oz oats (or a mixture
of buckwheat and large oats)
100g/3½oz mixed seeds (pumpkin,
sunflower, sesame, flax and poppy)
100g/3½oz mixed nuts, coarsely chopped
1 tsp salt

flavourings
2 tsp ground cinnamon
200g/7oz dried fruit, chopped

sweeteners
200g/7oz apple or other fruit compote
(see recipes pages 30–35) – put the
compote through a blender
if it contains too many pieces
200g/7oz agave or maple syrup,
or golden syrup
2 tbsp sunflower oil

Preheat the oven to 150°C/300°F/Gas mark 2. Prepare the sweeteners first. Heat the fruit compote, syrup and sunflower oil in a saucepan until the mixture becomes runny. Stir all the dry ingredients together, apart from the dried fruit which is added at the end. Stir in all the remaining ingredients.

Spread the granola mixture over two baking sheets. Bake in the oven for about 45 minutes, stirring every 10 minutes, until nice and golden. Remove the granola from the oven and leave to cool. Stir in the dried fruit. Store the granola in an airtight tin.

granola

citrus fruit granola

Create an explosion of citrus flavours with this luscious blend of candied orange and lemon, orange zest, Grapefruit and Orange Compote and orange marmalade.

makes about 1kg/2¼lbs • preparation time: 10 minutes • cooking time: 45 minutes

oat base
5 quantities Muesli with Nuts & Seeds
(see recipe page 49)

alternative base
350g/12oz oats (mixture of buckwheat
and large oats)
100g/3½oz mixed seeds (pumpkin,
sunflower, sesame, flax and poppy)
100g/3½oz mixed nuts, coarsely chopped
1 tsp salt

flavourings
50g/1¾oz candied orange, chopped
50g/1¾oz candied lemon, chopped
Zest of 2 oranges, finely grated

sweeteners
150g/5½oz Grapefruit & Orange
Compote *(see recipe page 20)* – put the
compote through a blender
if it contains too many pieces
200g/7oz honey
100g/3½oz orange marmalade
2 tbsp sunflower oil

Preheat the oven to 160°C/312°F/Gas mark 2–3. First prepare the sweeteners. Heat the fruit compote, honey, marmalade and sunflower oil in a saucepan until the mixture becomes runny. Stir in all the dry ingredients, apart from the candied fruit and orange zest, which are added at the end.

Spread the granola mixture over two baking sheets. Bake in the oven for about 45 minutes, stirring every 10 minutes, until nice and golden. Remove from the oven and leave to cool.

Stir in the candied fruits and orange zest. Store the granola in an airtight tin.

granola with far-eastern flavours

Preserved ginger, sesame seeds, cashews and plum compote bring the favours of the East to this granola.

makes about 1kg/2¼lb • preparation time: 10 minutes • cooking time: 45 minutes

oat base
300g/10½oz oats (mixture of buckwheat and large oats)
50g/1¾oz sunflower seeds
25g/1oz golden sesame seeds
25g/1oz black sesame seeds
50g/1¾oz pumpkin seeds
150g/5½oz cashews, coarsely chopped
1 tsp salt

flavourings
50g/1¾oz preserved ginger, finely chopped
150g/5½oz prunes, chopped

sweeteners
250g/9oz Plum & Ginger Compote *(see recipe page 31)* – put the compote through a blender if it contains too many pieces
250g/9oz palm sugar or honey
2 tbsp sunflower oil

Preheat the oven to 150°C/300°F/Gas mark 2. Prepare the sweeteners first. Heat the fruit compote, syrup and sunflower oil in a saucepan until the mixture becomes runny. Stir all the dry ingredients together, apart from the flavourings, which are added at the end. Stir in all the remaining ingredients.

Spread the granola mixture over two baking sheets. Bake in the oven for about 45 minutes, stirring every 10 minutes, until nice and golden. Remove the granola from the oven and leave to cool.

Stir in the dried fruit. Store the granola in an airtight tin.

crunchy honey granola

*Francesca Unsworth was my culinary collaborator until she moved to Australia.
We often went out together in Paris to discover the city's gastronomic delights.
This recipe was inspired by the Sonoma Café in Sydney – the Paddington
neighbourhood's branch of the famous Australian artisan bakery – where
she liked to go for a morning energy top-up.*

*makes about 1kg/2¼lb • preparation time: 10 minutes •
cooking time: 45 minutes*

oat base
360g/12oz oats (mixture of buckwheat
and large oats)
100g/3½oz almonds, coarsely chopped
100g/10½oz walnuts, coarsely chopped
1 tsp salt

flavourings
2 tsp ground cinnamon
150g/5½oz sultanas

sweeteners
250g/9oz honey
2 tbsp sunflower oil

Preheat the oven to 160°C/312°F/Gas mark 2–3. First prepare the sweeteners.
Heat the honey and sunflower oil in a saucepan until the mixture becomes runny.
Add all the dry ingredients, apart from sultanas, which are added at the end, and
stir well.

Spread the granola mixture over two baking sheets. Bake in the oven for about
45 minutes, stirring every 10 minutes, until nice and golden. Remove from the
oven and leave to cool.

Stir in the sultanas. Store the granola in an airtight tin.

triple chocolate gluten-free granola

What this granola lacks in gluten, it makes up for in chocolate.

makes about 1kg/2¼lb • preparation time: 10 minutes • cooking time: 45 minutes

cereal flake granola base
300g/10½oz buckwheat oats
120g/4oz millet oats
150g/5½oz buckwheat flakes
25g/1oz puffed rice
25g/1oz puffed quinoa
50g/1¾oz cocoa nibs
(cocoa beans roasted and shelled)
1 tsp salt

flavourings
100g/3½oz dark chocolate,
coarsely chopped

100g/3½oz milk chocolate,
coarsely chopped
100g/3½oz white chocolate,
coarsely chopped

sweeteners
300g/10½oz agave or maple syrup,
honey or golden syrup
2 tbsp sunflower oil
50g/1¾oz cocoa powder

Preheat the oven to 160°C/312°F/Gas mark 2–3. First prepare the sweeteners. Heat the agave, maple syrup, honey or golden syrup with the sunflower oil and cocoa powder in a saucepan until the mixture becomes runny. Add all the dry ingredients, apart from the three kinds of chocolate, which are added at the end, and stir well.

Spread the granola mixture over two baking sheets. Bake in the oven for about 45 minutes, stirring every 10 minutes, until nice and golden. Remove from the oven and leave to cool. Stir the chocolate into the mixture. Store the granola in an airtight tin.

PORRIDGE

traditional porridge

In Scotland, porridge is traditionally made with oats, water and salt. Cream or cold milk is served on the side to create a contrast between hot and cold. My favourite way of making porridge is to use milk instead of water and sweeten it with a generous dash of maple syrup.

serves 1 • preparation time: 10 minutes • cooking time: 20–30 minutes

50g/1¾oz oats (for a really creamy porridge choose small oat flakes)
300–400ml/½ pint–14fl oz water, half-and-half water and milk or milk only
1 tbsp honey or sweetener of your choice (optional)
25ml/1fl oz chilled single cream, for serving (optional)
Pinch salt

Toast the oats in a small, heavy-based saucepan for 2–3 minutes stirring constantly with a wooden spoon. Gradually add the liquid (water, water and milk, or milk only) and salt, then reduce the heat and cook, stirring from time to time, for 20–30 minutes, according to whether you like your porridge thin or thick. If it thickens too much, just add a little more water or milk.

Drizzle with honey or your choice of sweetener. Serve with chilled cream, if desired, and fruit compote or stewed or fresh fruit.

Persian porridge

What makes this porridge special is its delicious garnish – fruit compote, fresh fruit or nuts ... the choice is yours.

---

*serves 1 • preparation time: **5 minutes** • cooking time: **55 minutes***

50g/1¾oz pearl barley
500ml/16fl oz water
1 tbsp flaked almonds
175ml/6fl oz milk
2 tsp honey
1 tsp rose water
4 tbsp Apricot & Date Compote with Rose Water (see recipe page 35)
Pinch salt

Put the pearl barley and water in a large saucepan and bring to the boil. Lower the heat and simmer for 25–35 minutes or until soft. Drain thoroughly.

Toast the flaked almonds in a dry frying pan for 1–2 minutes. Wash the saucepan used for the pearl barley, then mix the pearl barley, milk, salt and honey in the saucepan. Bring to the boil, then lower the heat and simmer for 10–15 minutes.

Remove from the heat and stir in the rose water. Garnish with the compote and toasted almonds. Add milk and sugar if you wish.

chicken congee

The first time I tasted this savoury porridge was at breakfast in my grandmother's home in Malaysia. When I was a child my mother preferred to serve it as a quick supper. I rarely roast a whole chicken, which is why my recipe starts from scratch. However, if you have some leftovers handy, this is a delicious way of using them up.

*serves 2 • preparation time: **30 minutes** • cooking time: **30 minutes***

1 red chilli, deseeded and finely sliced
4 tbsp soy sauce
2 tbsp sunflower or vegetable oil (not olive oil)
1 chicken thigh
2 tsp garlic, finely chopped
2 tsp fresh ginger, finely grated
1 star anise
1 tbsp fish sauce or 1 anchovy fillet
2 spring onions, chopped
1.5 litres/2½ pints boiling water
100g/3½oz short-grain or risotto rice
4 tbsp tinned sweetcorn
1 tbsp sesame oil
Salt
Black pepper

Put the chilli in a small bowl with the soy sauce. Heat the oil in a large, non-stick frying pan. Place the chicken thigh in the pan, skin side down. Fry for about 4 minutes on each side until golden. When you turn the chicken over, add the garlic, ginger, star anise, fish sauce or anchovy and the white part of the spring onions (keep the green for garnishing). Add the boiling water (take care as it may splash), cover the pan and simmer for 30 minutes.

Wash the rice and place it in a small saucepan. Remove the chicken from the frying pan and wrap it in foil. Pour the cooking liquid through a fine sieve into a jug or bowl, then add to the saucepan containing the rice.

Cook the rice for about 20 minutes or according to instructions on the pack. The congee should be thick and creamy. If it's too dry, add a little boiling water. Bone the chicken thigh and cut the meat into strips. Season the rice with salt and pepper and divide it between two bowls. Garnish each serving with the green part of the spring onions, sweetcorn, chicken strips, a few drops of sesame oil and a few drops of the chilli-infused soy sauce (optional).

quick version
Use ready-made chicken stock and buy a roast chicken thigh. Briefly brown the garlic, ginger and spring onions with the rice for 2 minutes. Add the chicken stock and follow the recipe from cooking the rice.

porridge

80

porridge

rice pudding

If your child isn't too keen on milk, it's a good idea to make him or her milk-based desserts, like rice pudding. Topped up with fruit compote, chopped dried fruit or a spot of jam, rice pudding is a treat for all ages.

serves 10 children or 2 adults • preparation time: 15 minutes • cooking time: 30 minutes

1 vanilla pod
80g/3oz short-grain, risotto or pudding rice
450ml/15fl oz milk
(for a creamier version use 200ml/7fl oz single cream and 250ml/8fl oz milk)
1 tsp sugar

Split the vanilla pod, scrape out the seeds and put them, together with the pod, into a saucepan with the rice and milk. Bring to the boil, then simmer for 25–30 minutes or until the rice softens. Remove the vanilla pod and stir in the sugar. Serve hot or cold.

If you refrigerate rice pudding, you may need to add a little milk before serving as it has a tendency to harden as it cools.

MUESLI BARS

classic muesli bar

A classic muesli bar contains oat flakes, nuts and dried fruit, as well as oil and sugar syrup to hold it all together. Have fun trying out different combinations of ingredients to create your favourite muesli bar.

makes 12 bars • preparation time: 10 minutes • cooking time: 20–30 minutes

muesli bar base
275g/9¾oz oats
100g/3½oz dried fruit
50g/1¾oz nuts, chopped
25g/1oz mixed seeds
50g/1¾oz sunflower seeds

alternative base
5 quantities Muesli Base (see recipe page 39)

sweeteners
2 tbsp palm or golden caster sugar
120g/4oz agave, maple or golden syrup
80ml/2½fl oz vegetable oil

Preheat the oven to 170°C/325°F/Gas mark 3. First prepare the sweeteners. Dissolve the sugar with the syrup and oil in a saucepan over a medium heat. Stir all the dry ingredients together then stir in the sugar syrup.

Line a rectangular cake tin, measuring about 20 x 25cm/8 x 10in, with greaseproof paper. Pour the mixture into the tin and spread it across the entire surface. For crunchy muesli bars, bake for 25–30 minutes. If you prefer them softer, only bake them for 20 minutes.

Leave to cool for 10 minutes, then cut into rectangles while the muesli is still warm, otherwise it will be difficult to cut. Store in airtight tins.

If using the muesli base, prepare the sweeteners and mix with the muesli base. Follow the baking instructions as above.

'no-cook' muesli bar

These bars are easy to make and need no cooking – just a simple blend of dried fruit and nuts, plus oats for a crunchier texture. They are also an excellent source of natural sugars, fibre and omega-3 – ideal food for mind and body.

*makes 6–8 bars • preparation time: 15 minutes •
resting time: 4 hours or overnight*

150g/5½oz date paste*
100g/3½oz dried apricots
50g/1¾oz dried figs
200g/7oz mixed nuts or pulp left over
after making Nut Milk (see page 22)
80g/2¾oz oat flakes or ground almonds
Pinch salt

Pinch ground cinnamon
Pinch ground ginger
Vegetable oil

** Date paste is available from
healthfood shops or North African
or Middle Eastern grocers.*

Put all the ingredients into a blender or food-processor and blend for a few moments at a time, until the nuts are chopped into small pieces and well combined with the date paste. If you are using nut pulp, add it after you have blended the fruit and nuts.

Grease the base and sides of a small rectangular tin with a little oil. Fill the tin with the date mixture and tap down gently with your hand or the back of a spoon to achieve a smooth, even layer. Leave in the refrigerator overnight.

Divide into 5 or 6 bars, or as many portions as you want. Use a pastry cutter if you like. The bars will keep for about a week in an airtight container.

variations
Omit the spices and add 1 tbsp rose water for a Middle Eastern flavour or 1 tbsp preserved ginger for a Far Eastern touch. These muesli bars are also very good with 1 tbsp finely grated orange zest.

cherry & pistachio muesli bar

This is a more sophisticated muesli bar with red cherries and green pistachios to add a splash of colour.

makes 12 bars • preparation time: 10 minutes • cooking time: 20–30 minutes

2 tbsp golden caster sugar
120g/4oz agave, maple or golden syrup
80ml/2½fl oz vegetable oil
350g/12oz oat flakes
100g/3½oz fresh or tinned cherries, stoned
50g/1¾oz shelled pistachios

Preheat the oven to 170°C/325°F/Gas mark 3. Dissolve the sugar with the syrup and oil in a saucepan over a medium heat. Stir all the dry ingredients together then stir in the sugar syrup. Line a rectangular cake tin, measuring about 20 x 25cm/8 x 10in, with greaseproof paper. Pour the mixture into the tin and spread it across the entire surface. Bake for 20–30 minutes.

Leave to cool for 10 minutes, then cut into rectangles while the muesli is still warm, otherwise it will be difficult to cut. Store in airtight tins.

salted caramel & nut muesli bar

This salty-sweet muesli bar might sound strange at first, but it tastes very much like caramel made with salted butter. You could quickly become addicted to the combination of caramel flavours and peanut butter.

makes 12 bars • preparation time: 10 minutes • cooking time: 20–30 minutes

100g/3½oz peanut butter
80g/3oz maple or golden syrup
80g/3oz caramel sweets
375g/13oz oats
50g/1¾oz peanuts, chopped
50g/1¾oz cashews, chopped
25g/1oz pine nuts
1 tsp salt

Preheat the oven to 170°C/325°F/Gas mark 3. Dissolve the peanut butter, syrup and caramel sweets in a saucepan over a medium heat. Stir all the dry ingredients together then stir in the sugar syrup. Line a rectangular cake tin, measuring about 20 x 25cm/8 x 10in, with greaseproof paper. Pour the mixture into the tin and spread it across the entire surface.

For crunchy muesli bars, bake for 25–30 minutes. If you prefer them softer, only bake for 20 minutes. Leave to cool for 10 minutes then cut into rectangles while the muesli is still warm, otherwise it will be difficult to cut. Store in airtight tins.

light gluten-free
muesli bar

In this reduced-sugar, low-fat muesli bar, egg white replaces vegetable oil and bananas replace some of the sugar. It also uses buckwheat flakes and puffed rice, making it gluten-free.

makes 12 bars • preparation time: 10 minutes • cooking time: 20–30 minutes

2 ripe bananas, mashed
80g/3oz agave syrup
1 egg white
150g/5½oz buckwheat flakes
100g/3½oz Rice Krispies or puffed rice
1 tsp cinnamon

Preheat the oven to 170°C/325°F/Gas mark 3. Mix together the bananas, syrup and egg white, then stir them straight into the dry ingredients. Line a rectangular cake tin, measuring about 20 x 25cm/8 x 10in, with greaseproof paper. Pour the mixture into the tin and spread it across the entire surface. Bake for 20–30 minutes.

Leave to cool for 10 minutes, then cut into rectangles while the muesli is still warm, otherwise it will be difficult to cut. Store in airtight tins.

high-energy muesli bar

Packed with energy-giving ingredients, this muesli bar is perfect for when you are feeling tired. Ginger is a wonderful stimulant, while seeds, nuts, oat flakes and cranberries all provide vital nutrients that your body can't do without.

makes 12 bars • preparation time: 10 minutes • cooking time: 20–30 minutes

2 tbsp palm or golden caster sugar
120g/4oz agave syrup
80ml/2½fl oz vegetable oil
270g/9½oz oats
80g/3oz dried cranberries
30g/1oz preserved ginger, finely chopped
20g/¾oz mixed seeds
50g/1¾oz pumpkin seeds
50g/1¾oz almonds, coarsely chopped

Preheat the oven to 175°C/325°F/Gas mark 3. Dissolve the sugar with the syrup and oil in a saucepan over a medium heat. Stir all the dry ingredients together, then stir in the sugar syrup.

Line a rectangular cake tin, measuring about 20 x 25cm/8 x 10in, with greaseproof paper. Pour the mixture into the tin and spread it across the entire surface. Bake for 20–30 minutes.

Leave to cool for 10 minutes then cut into rectangles while the muesli is still warm, otherwise it will be difficult to cut. Store in airtight tins.

spicy chocolate muesli bar

The combination of chocolate and chilli pepper is very popular in Mexico. Chilli powder adds a spicy kick to this muesli bar. Increase or reduce the suggested quantity to taste.

makes 12 bars • preparation time: 10 minutes • cooking time: 20–30 minutes

120g/4oz palm or golden caster sugar
80ml/2½fl oz vegetable oil
400g/14oz oats
130g/4½oz dark chocolate, coarsely chopped
75g/2¾oz almonds, coarsely chopped
1 tsp chilli powder

Preheat the oven to 170°C/325°F/Gas mark 3. Dissolve the sugar in the oil in a saucepan over a medium heat. Stir all the dry ingredients together, then stir in the sugar syrup.

Line a rectangular cake tin, measuring about 20 x 25cm/8 x 10in, with greaseproof paper. Pour the mixture into the tin and spread it across the entire surface. Bake for 20–30 minutes.

Leave to cool for 10 minutes then cut into rectangles while the muesli is still warm, otherwise it will be difficult to cut. Store in airtight tins.

double chocolate flapjacks

Like granola bars, flapjacks contain lots of oat flakes. The difference is that they also contain the delicious combination of butter and golden syrup. Enjoy them as a teatime treat.

makes 12 bars • preparation time: 15 minutes • cooking time: 20–30 minutes

100g/3½oz butter
150g/5½oz dark chocolate
150g/5½oz golden syrup
450g/1lb oats

to decorate
100g/3½oz white chocolate
1 tbsp single cream

Preheat the oven to 170°C/325°F/Gas mark 3. Melt the butter, chocolate and syrup in a saucepan over a medium heat. Stir the mixture into the oat flakes. Line a rectangular cake tin, measuring about 20 x 25cm/8 x 10in, with greaseproof paper. Pour the mixture into the tin and spread it across the entire surface. Bake for 20–30 minutes.

Leave to cool for 10 minutes, then cut into rectangles while the muesli is still warm, otherwise it will be difficult to cut.

Put the white chocolate and single cream in a glass or metal bowl and place over a saucepan of simmering water. When the chocolate has melted, drizzle the mixture over the flapjacks. Store the flapjacks in an airtight tin.

A FEW MORE IDEAS

muesli balls

Bite-sized portions of muesli mixed with dried fruit and butter that you won't be able to stop eating.

makes 24 balls • preparation time: 20 minutes • cooking time: 5 minutes

200g/7oz toasted oats
175g/6oz dried apricots, dates or figs
40g/1½oz butter, melted

Put the oats, dried fruit and warm melted butter into a food-processor. Blend for 2–3 minutes or until thoroughly mixed. Shape the mixture into bite-sized balls.

Refrigerate in an airtight container for at least 4 hours. Muesli balls will keep in the refrigerator for up to a week.

a few more ideas

muesli & chocolate truffles

A slightly more elaborate version of muesli balls. With the addition of chocolate and pistachios they could even pass as chocolate truffles.

makes 24 balls • preparation time: 20 minutes • cooking time: 10 minutes

100g/3½oz chocolate
175g/6oz dried apricots, dates or figs
200g/7oz toasted oats
50g/1¾oz pistachios, finely chopped

Put the chocolate in a glass or metal bowl and place it over a saucepan of simmering water until the chocolate has melted. The bowl should not touch the water. Put the dried fruit and oats in a food-processor. Blend for 2–3 minutes or until mixed thoroughly, then stir into the melted chocolate. Shape the mixture into bite-sized balls, then roll in the chopped pistachios to coat.

Refrigerate in an airtight container for at least 4 hours. The truffles will keep in the refrigerator for up to a week.

muesli bread rolls

This recipe calls for two types of spelt flour. Wholemeal spelt flour brings depth while white spelt flour adds a lighter touch. For a more rustic bread, replace the white flour with wholemeal.

makes 12 rolls • preparation time: 30 minutes • proving time: 2 hours • cooking time: 30–40 minutes

150ml/5fl oz milk

50g/1¾oz plain yogurt

130ml/4fl oz hot water

30g/1oz honey

20g/¾oz fresh yeast (you can buy fresh yeast from your local bakery).

100g/3½oz Muesli Base *(see recipe page 39)*

200g/7oz stone-ground wholemeal spelt flour

200g/7oz white spelt flour

2 tsp salt

60g/2oz dried apricots, roughly chopped

60g/2oz dried dates, roughly chopped

60g/2oz hazelnuts, roughly chopped

30g/1oz pistachios, shelled

1 egg, beaten

oats or muesli, for sprinkling

Combine the milk and yogurt, then add the hot water and honey – the mixture should be lukewarm. Stir in the yeast. When the yeast has dissolved add the muesli. Cover and leave to stand in a warm place until the yeast starts to bubble (about 15–20 minutes).

Sift the two types of flour and add the salt. Add the milk, yogurt and yeast mixture to the flour and stir well. The dough should be slightly sticky. Knead it on a floured surface for about 5 minutes, until you have an even texture. Stretch the dough into a rectangle and sprinkle with the dried fruit, hazelnuts and pistachios. Knead for a further 4–5 minutes until the fruit and nuts are evenly spread through the dough. Shape the dough into a ball and place in a lightly oiled container. Cover with a damp tea towel and leave to prove in a warm, draught-free place for 1 hour or until the dough has doubled in size.

Place the dough on a floured surface and divide into 12 equal-sized portions. Shape into small balls then arrange them in a greased baking tin lined with greaseproof paper. Brush the rolls with beaten egg and sprinkle with oats or muesli. Cover with aluminium foil and leave to prove for another 30 minutes.

Preheat the oven to 220°C/425°F/Gas mark 7. Bake the rolls for 30–40 minutes until golden. If they brown too quickly, cover with aluminium foil. Remove from the oven and leave to cool on a grid.

muesli cookies

These are my favourite cookies – the oat flakes make them soft on the inside and crunchy on the outside.

makes 25–35 cookies • preparation time: 15 minutes • cooking time: 20 minutes

basic cookie dough
225g/8oz golden caster sugar
225g/8oz butter, softened
2 eggs
150g/5½oz plain flour

325g/11¼oz oats
1 tsp baking powder

flavourings
200g/7oz chocolate, fresh or dried fruit, nuts or a combination of all

Preheat the oven to 170°C/325°F/Gas mark 3. Rub the sugar and butter together, then beat in the eggs, one at a time. In a separate bowl, mix together the flour, oats and baking powder, then add the chocolate (or other chosen ingredient) to flavour the cookies. Stir all the ingredients to a smooth dough.

Line a baking tray with greaseproof paper. Shape the dough into cookies using an ice cream scoop or large spoon. Arrange the cookies on the baking tray about 5cm/2in apart and flatten them slightly. Bake for 15–20 minutes or until golden.

To enjoy freshly baked cookies at any time of day, prepare a large quantity of dough, shape into cookies, then keep them in an airtight tin in the refrigerator for up to a week or in the freezer for up to 2 months.

more ideas for flavourings
You can add the following combinations of ingredients to the basic cookie dough:
Cranberry and orange: 200g/7oz cranberries and the grated zest of 1 orange.
Apple and cinnamon: 200g/7oz apples, peeled and diced and 2 tsp ground cinnamon.
Banana, walnut and chocolate: 50g/1¾oz banana, 50g/1¾oz walnuts and 100g/3½oz chocolate, chopped.

Bob's smoothie & mini muesli muffins

These are perfect breakfast muffins – not too sweet with a delicious banana flavour. Bob, aka Marc Grossman, is the author of several recipe books including Smoothie *and owner of Bob's Juice Bar and Bob's Kitchen in Paris. The smoothie recipe is his.*

Bob's muesli smoothie

serves 2

300ml/10fl oz almond milk
1 ripe banana, peeled and deep-frozen
75g/2¾oz berries, fresh or frozen
1½ tbsp small oats
1 tbsp agave or maple syrup

Put all the ingredients together in a blender and blend until creamy.
If your blender isn't powerful enough, don't use a frozen banana and
serve the smoothie with ice cubes instead.

mini muesli muffins

makes 12 muffins • *preparation time: 20 minutes* •
cooking time: 30 minutes

125g/4½oz yogurt
2 eggs
1 tsp vanilla essence
50g/1¾oz banana chips
(soft, not the chewy type)
100g/3½oz Muesli Base
(see recipe page 39)
100g/3½oz softened butter

100g/3½oz unrefined sugar
1 large banana (as ripe as possible – if
you use just-ripe bananas, the texture of
the muffin will be too moist and doughy)
200g/7oz flour
3 tsp baking powder
10g/¼oz oats, for sprinkling

Preheat the oven to 180°C/350°F/Gas mark 4. Place paper muffin cases in a muffin tin. Whisk the yogurt with the eggs and vanilla essence, then add the banana chips and muesli. Leave to soak for a few minutes so that they absorb the liquid. Work the butter and sugar together until fluffy. Chop the ripe banana into small pieces and add to the butter mixture. Stir into the yogurt mixture.

Sift the flour and baking powder. Stir the butter and yogurt mixture into the flour. Important: don't stir too much – muffins turn out better when the dough is slightly lumpy. Fill the muffin cases with the dough. Sprinkle the oats on top.

Bake for 30 minutes or until the muffins are golden and spring back when you press them gently with your finger. Remove the muffins from the tin and leave to cool on a rack. Muffins are best eaten warm or at least on the day they are made. Uncooked muffin dough can be frozen. Defrost overnight in the refrigerator then bake in the oven as above.

a few more ideas

muesli crumble

Crumble is a typically British pudding. During the Second World War, baking ingredients were difficult to come by and cooks had to make do with the small rations of flour, sugar and butter they were allowed. So they invented crumble, a pudding composed of fruit baked in the oven with a crisp, crumbly topping – hence the name. Delicious served with crème Anglaise – or custard, as it's known in the UK.

serves 4–6 • preparation time: 15 minutes • cooking time: 30 minutes

crumble topping
100g/3½oz wholemeal flour
50g/1¾oz golden caster sugar
80g/3oz oats
100g/3½oz butter, chilled and diced

fruit filling
500g/1lb 2oz fruit of your choice
50g/1¾oz golden caster sugar or sweetener of your choice

Preheat the oven to 180°C/350°F/Gas mark 4. Combine the flour, sugar and oats. Add the diced butter. Work the ingredients together with your fingertips to achieve a crumbly, sandy texture.

Stone or core the fruit and chop into large pieces. Mix the fruit and sugar and spread over the base of a large ovenproof dish. Sprinkle the crumble topping over the fruit. Bake for 25–30 minutes or until the crumble is golden.

variations

You can also make a delicious crumble with fruit compote (see recipes on pages 30–35, apart from Apricot & Date Compote with Rose Water). You can even use a mixture of different compotes. For example, combine Plum & Ginger Compote with Grapefruit & Orange Compote. To add flavour to the crumble topping, use 40g/1½oz ground almonds or pulp left over from making Nut Milk (see page 22).

a few more ideas

crème Anglaise

makes about 500ml/17floz • preparation time: 10 minutes • cooking time: 25 minutes

250ml/8fl oz milk
250ml/8fl oz single cream
1 vanilla pod
2 egg yolks
80g/3oz sugar

Pour the milk and cream into a saucepan. Split the vanilla pod lengthways, scrape out the seeds and add to the saucepan. Add the vanilla pod and bring to the boil.

Mix the egg yolks and sugar. Slowly pour the hot milk and cream mixture over the egg yolks, stirring constantly to prevent the eggs from congealing. Return the mixture to the saucepan and continue to stir until it comes to the boil.

When the crème Anglaise has thickened a little, turn off the heat and discard the vanilla pod. Serve hot with the crumble or refrigerate in an airtight container. Crème Anglaise will keep in the refrigerator for up to one week.

syllabub with citrus fruit granola

Syllabub is a classic British dessert based on cream or full-fat milk, lightly curdled with wine or cider. It has a light, creamy texture in perfect contrast to the crunchy granola. For a non-alcoholic version, use apple juice instead of wine.

serves 4–6 • preparation time: 15 minutes • chilling time: 1 hour

syllabub
1 lemon
(preferably unwaxed or organic)
50g/1¾oz caster sugar
50ml/1½fl oz sweet white wine
or Madeira (or apple juice for a
non-alcoholic version)
250ml/8fl oz double cream

granola
80g/3oz Citrus Fruit Granola
(see recipe page 63)

Finely grate the lemon zest. Reserve half to decorate the syllabub and put the rest in a saucepan. Squeeze the juice from the lemon into the saucepan, add the sugar, then cook over a medium heat until the sugar has dissolved. Add the wine, Madeira or apple juice.

Whip the cream until it forms peaks. Slowly pour the lemon mixture over the cream, continuing to whip.

Divide the granola between 4–6 glasses. Top with the cream and lemon mixture and leave in the refrigerator to chill for at least 1 hour. Sprinkle with the reserved lemon zest before serving.

a few more ideas

granola, strawberry and chocolate trifle

Trifle is another traditional pudding, usually consisting of a génoise sponge cake base covered with layers of custard and fruit and topped with whipped cream. This recipe uses granola instead of the génoise, adding a wonderful touch of crunchiness.

serves 4–6 • preparation time: 15 minutes • chilling time: 1 hour

120ml/4fl oz double or whipping cream
1 sachet vanilla sugar
100g/3½oz Triple Chocolate Gluten-free Granola *(see recipe page 69)*
200g/7oz cold Crème Anglaise *(see recipe page 117)*
100g/3½oz strawberries, cut into quarters
Chocolate flakes or chocolate vermicelli

Whip the cream and vanilla sugar until firm. Fill 4–6 glasses with alternating layers of granola, crème Anglaise and strawberries, finishing with a layer of cream. Sprinkle with chocolate flakes or chocolate vermicelli and serve immediately. The trifle can be prepared 1 hour in advance and left to chill in the refrigerator.

index

index

127

index